T0403078

**X-TREME FACTS: ENGINEERING**

# TUNNELS

by Catherine C. Finan

**BEARPORT**
PUBLISHING

Minneapolis, Minnesota

## Credits:

Cover and title page, Metropolitan Transportation Authority/Patrick Cashin/Creative Commons; 4 top left, Blue Peep/Creative Commons; 4 top, Idawriter/Creative Commons; 4 bottom left, T.TATSU/Shutterstock; 4 bottom right, Honza Groh/Creative Commons; 5 top, H.L.I.T/Creative Commons; 5 top middle, taviphoto/Shutterstock.com; 5 top left, right, Chalermphon Srisang/Shutterstock; 5 middle, Bmazerolles/Creative Commons; 5 bottom, Störfix/Creative Commons; 5 bottom left, Sorn340 Studio Images/Shutterstock; 5 bottom right, Dragana Gordic/Shutterstock; 6 top, Édouard BERGÉ/Creative Commons; 6 top left, Einsamer Schütze/Creative Commons; 6 bottom, Gorgo/Public Domain; 7 top, British Museum/Public Domain; 7 top left, Albert Kretschmer and Dr. Carl Rohrbach/Public Domain; 7 top right, James Tissot/Public Domain; 7 bottom, Tamar Hayardeni/Creative Commons; 7 bottom left, 11 bottom right, 25 bottom right, 27 top middle, LightField Studios/Shutterstock; 7 bottom middle, Andrey Arkusha /Shutterstock; 7 bottom right Davidbena/Creative Commons; 8 top, Diego Delso/Creative Commons; 8 bottom, Krzysztof Golik/Creative Commons; 8 bottom left, Roberto Bompiani/Public Domain; 8 bottom middle, A. Pigma/Public Domain; 9 top, 1881: acquired by William T. Walters/Public Domain; 9 top left, Eric Isselee/Shutterstock; 9 bottom, Gianfranco Vitolo/Creative Commons; 9 bottom left, engagestock/Shutterstock; 9 bottom middle, Public Domain; 9 bottom right, meunierd/Shutterstock; 10–11, 11 top, Rijin/Creative Commons; 10 top, Dancorona21/Creative Commons; 10 bottom right, Marko Poplasen/Shutterstock; 11 top right, ViDI Studio/Shutterstock; 11 bottom left, Jeka/Shutterstock; 12 bottom, Public Domain; 12 bottom left, James Northcote/Public Domain; 13 top, Swain/Public Domain; 13 bottom, Lars Plougmann/Creative Commons; 13 bottom middle, Max_555/Shutterstock; 13 bottom left, Gorodenkoff/Shutterstock; 14 Rhododendrites/Creative Commons; 14 left, George Grantham Bain Collection/Public Domain; 15 top, testing/Shutterstock.com; 15 middle, MNXANL/Creative Commons; 15 bottom top, peiyang/Shutterstock; 15 bottom far left, Lucy.Brown/Shutterstock.com; 15 bottom left, Miguel/Creative Commons; 15 bottom middle, Joe Tabacca/Shutterstock; 15 bottom right, Ralf Roletschek/Creative Commons; 16 top, Roland zh/Creative Commons; 16 bottom, Edward Villiers Rippingille/Public Domain; 17 top, SounderBruce/Creative Commons; 17 top right, Asahel Curtis/Public Domain; 17 bottom, MikeDotta/Shutterstock; 17 bottom right, Alis Photo/Shutterstock; 18 top, Tambo/Creative Commons; 18 bottom, myboys.me/Shutterstock; 19 top, Billy69150/Creative Commons; 19 top right, Natalia Yurkova/Shutterstock; 19 bottom, Kaca Skokanova/Shutterstock.com; 19 bottom right, fizkes/Shutterstock; 20 top, Hannes Ortlieb/Creative Commons; 20 middle, Kecko/Creative Commons; 20 middle right, CGN089/Shutterstock; 20 bottom, blazg/Shutterstock; 21 top, vastateparksstaff/Creative Commons; 21 top right, Dragon Images/Shutterstock; 21 middle, Jana Janina/Shutterstock; 21 bottom, gringos4/Shutterstock; 21 bottom left, Anna Om/Shutterstock; 21 bottom right, Inside Creative House/Shutterstock; 22 top, Zairon/Creative Commons; 22 top middle, Dimitris Leonidas/Shutterstock; 22 bottom, Alex Proimos/Creative Commons; 23 top, Patrick Pelster/Creative Commons; 23 top right, Executive Office of the President of the United States/Public Domain; 23 middle, Duane Howell/The Denver Post via Getty Images; 23 bottom, FANG Chen/Creative Commons; 24 top, WeHaKa/Creative Commons; 24 top left, Prostock-studio/Shutterstock; 24 top right, paffy/Shutterstock; 24–25 bottom, sirtravelalot/Shutterstock; 24 bottom left, Jeka/Shutterstock; 25 top, JMK/Creative Commons; 25 top left, Roman Samborskyi/Shutterstock; 25 top right, ViDI Studio/Shutterstock; 25 bottom left, Nutlegal Photographer/Shutterstock; 26, Jeangagnon/Creative Commons; 26 bottom left, DavideAngelini/Shutterstock; 26 bottom right, paffy/Shutterstock; 27 top, Ami Parikh/Shutterstock; 27 bottom, f11photo/Shutterstock; 27 bottom middle, Syda Productions/Shutterstock; 28 top, http://www.cgpgrey.com/Creative Commons; 28 middle left, Frank Schulenburg/CC BY-SA 4.0; 28 bottom left, Zacharie Grossen/Creative Commons; 28–29, Austen Photography

**Bearport Publishing Company Product Development Team**
President: Jen Jenson; Director of Product Development: Spencer Brinker; Senior Editor: Allison Juda; Editor: Charly Haley; Associate Editor: Naomi Reich; Senior Designer: Colin O'Dea; Associate Designer: Elena Klinkner; Product Development Assistant: Anita Stasson

Produced for Bearport Publishing by BlueAppleWorks Inc.
Managing Editor for BlueAppleWorks: Melissa McClellan
Art Director: T.J. Choleva
Photo Research: Jane Reid

*Library of Congress Cataloging-in-Publication Data*

Names: Finan, Catherine C., 1972- author.
Title: Tunnels / by Catherine C. Finan.
Description: Minneapolis, Minnesota : Bearport Publishing Company, [2023] | Series: X-treme facts. Engineering | Includes bibliographical references and index.
Identifiers: LCCN 2022007036 (print) | LCCN 2022007037 (ebook) | ISBN 9798885091688 (library binding) | ISBN 9798885091756 (paperback) | ISBN 9798885091824 (ebook)
Subjects: LCSH: Tunnels--Juvenile literature.
Classification: LCC TA807 .F56 2023 (print) | LCC TA807 (ebook) | DDC 624.1/93--dc23/eng/20220217
LC record available at https://lccn.loc.gov/2022007036
LC ebook record available at https://lccn.loc.gov/2022007037

For more information, write to Bearport Publishing, 5357 Penn Avenue South, Minneapolis, MN 55419. Printed in the United States of America.

# Contents

# Can You Dig It?

Some of the greatest things ever built by humans are actually deep underground beneath our feet. What could they be? Tunnels! These tube-shaped passageways have allowed people to travel in ways that would otherwise be impossible. Holes made through stone or soil may seem simple at first glance. But tunnels are fantastic feats of **engineering**! Let's dig a little deeper . . .

The Holland Tunnel between New York and New Jersey was popular from the start. Almost 52,000 cars drove through the tunnel on its opening day in 1972.

LET'S JOIN THE CROWD!

OHHH, THAT'S WHERE THE WATER COMES FROM!

The next time you turn on a faucet, think about where the water comes from. Underground tunnels help carry water to people's homes.

In 1971, a railway **strike** stopped circus animals from reaching New York City by train. **So, instead, 19 elephants walked through the Lincoln Tunnel to get to their show!**

THE SHOW MUST GO ON!

Japan's Seikan railway tunnel is one of the world's deepest underwater tunnels. At 460 feet (140 m), it's deeper than the height of Egypt's Great Pyramid.

In the engineering world, **building a tunnel is called driving.**

Constructing tunnels often includes blasting **hard rock** with **explosives** and digging dirt with huge machines.

SO, IF YOU'LL JUST LOOK AT THE BUILDING PLANS . . .

DON'T YOU MEAN THE *DRIVING* PLANS?

# Ancient Tunnel Vision

Although building tunnels can be tricky, people have been doing it for thousands of years. The ancient Egyptians built some of the earliest tunnels about 4,700 years ago. These tunnel systems connected rooms beneath pyramids. **Archaeologists** believe the Mesopotamians made the first underwater tunnel beneath the Euphrates River a few centuries later. And those weren't the only groups to build tunnels long ago. Tunnels have dug their way through history!

Ancient Egyptians used saws made of copper and drills made from hollow reeds to carve tunnels into rock cliffs. That's some hard work . . . *literally!*

PHEW, I THINK I JUST EARNED MY LUNCH BREAK!

I SUPPOSE I KEPT MY SECRET LONG ENOUGH . . .

Archaeologists found a secret tunnel beneath the Pyramid of the Moon in Teotihuacan, Mexico. It was built more than 2,000 years ago.

The Mesopotamian tunnel below the Euphrates River **is believed to have been 3,000 ft (914 m) long.**

HOW DO I GET ACROSS THE RIVER?

USE THE TUNNEL. WE'VE JUST FINISHED IT!

To make the Euphrates tunnel, workers probably **diverted** the river, dug a **trench** across the riverbed, built a brick tunnel, and then let the river flow over it.

**Hezekiah's Tunnel was built 2,700 years ago to bring water into Jerusalem, Israel.** Today, you can walk through it—but you might get a little wet!

WOW, THIS IS SO OLD . . .

AND SO DAMP!

# Do as the Romans Do

Of all the people who built tunnels long ago, the ancient Romans made some that really stood out. Between about 300 BCE and 200 CE, they built huge stone structures called aqueducts to get water to people across the Roman Empire. The aqueducts were connected to a network of underground tunnels. And those were just some of the amazing tunnels in ancient Rome!

Rome's aqueducts were designed to use **gravity** and the **slope** of the land to move water downhill from lakes to cities.

About four-fifths of Rome's aqueduct system was made up of tunnels. That's a lot of tunnels!

RUN UP THAT HILL AND FETCH SOME WATER.

THERE'S NO NEED! THE AQUEDUCTS WILL BRING WATER TO US!

Water from the aqueducts was used for farming, drinking, and bathing—all things that we wouldn't want to live without!

Rome's Colosseum had tunnels below it. In ancient times, wild animals were lifted up from the tunnels onto a stage where they battled to the death.

WAIT, SO NOW WE'RE FIGHTING?!

YEAH—*YIKES!* AND I THOUGHT THAT DARK TUNNEL WAS GOING TO BE THE WORST PART!

The ancient Romans built the Pausilippo Tunnel in 36 BCE. The 4,800-ft (1.5-km) tunnel was dug through solid rock by hand.

Tunnels were also used to move pee and poop away from some ancient Roman cities.

THIS ISN'T THE TUNNEL THEY USE TO MOVE POOP AND PEE, IS IT?

WHAT A STINKY JOB!

NO, THANK GOODNESS! IT'S THE ONE THEY DUG BY HAND.

# Down in the Catacombs

Tunnels have been used to **transport** water, people, and more. But they've also been used for a much creepier purpose—as **catacombs** to house dead bodies! In the late 1700s, the city of Paris, France, ran out of space to bury people who died there. Their solution was to move more than 6 million dead bodies from overcrowded cemeteries into old **quarry** tunnels below the city. Today, you can walk through these catacombs . . . if you dare!

Bones line the walls of the catacombs. They're often arranged in patterns, such as circles, crosses, and hearts.

YOU CAME ALL THE WAY DOWN HERE TO SEE ME?

AHHH! NO, I THINK I TOOK A WRONG TURN! HOW DO I GET BACK TO THE CITY?

The Paris catacombs are about 65 ft (20 m) below the busy city.

One of the most famous bone patterns is called the Barrel. It supports its tunnel's ceiling and is made from skulls and leg bones.

IS THAT SKULL TALKING TO ME?!

THIS IS A REAL BARREL OF LAUGHS.

Together, the catacomb tunnels stretch for almost 200 miles (320 km).

OKAY, WE CAN GO A LITTLE FARTHER. BUT I'M NOT WALKING ALL 200 MILES OF THIS!

LET'S KEEP GOING!

More than half a million people visit the Paris catacombs each year.

# Under the River

Not long after Paris started using tunnels as catacombs, an engineering project in London, England, forever changed the way tunnels are constructed. The Thames Tunnel was built under the River Thames between 1825 and 1842. It was the world's first tunnel constructed beneath a flowing river without diverting the water. This was made possible by the invention of the tunneling shield, a structure that lets workers build a tunnel under a body of water without it caving in on them. Let's check it out!

Engineer Marc Brunel's tunneling shield invention was inspired by an animal called a shipworm. He saw one of these critters eating through a piece of rotted wood.

YOU'RE AN INSPIRATION!

AW, SHUCKS!

Today, the tunneling shield is a common tool for engineers around the world—all because of a pesky shipworm!

Building the Thames Tunnel was a slow process. Only about 8 to 12 ft (2.4 to 3.7 m) were finished each week.

WOO-HOO! THIS TUNNEL'S INCREDIBLE!

YEAH! WHO KNEW A TUNNEL COULD BE THIS FUN?!

The Thames Tunnel opened in 1843. About 50,000 people walked through it on the first day.

The tunnel's first visitors paid a penny each to walk through it.

Within 15 weeks of the tunnel being open, a million people had visited it.

Trains began running through the Thames Tunnel in the 1860s. The old tunnel is still part of London's rail system today.

THIS OLD TUNNEL STILL WORKS LIKE A CHARM!

# Super Subways

The Thames Tunnel isn't the only awesome tunnel in London. The city is also home to the world's first underground system of train tunnels, called the London Underground, which opened in 1863. Over in the United States, the oldest subway was built in Boston, Massachusetts, with train tunnels that opened in 1897. Not long after, New York City opened its famous subway system. These first underground trains offered a new way to get around busy cities—and changed public transportation forever!

On October 27, 1904, New York City Mayor George McClellan opened the subway by taking the controls of the first running train.

WHERE'S THE TRAIN? LET'S GET THIS SUBWAY GOING!

New York City's subway was built by digging the route near the surface, then supporting the sides and roof with beams and **columns** between the train tracks.

New York City has 472 train stations—the most of any subway system in the world!

The world's busiest subway system is in Beijing, China. Each day, about 9 million people ride the subway there. Now, that's a crowd!

HEY, COULD YOU GIVE ME A LITTLE ROOM HERE?

I WOULD IF I COULD . . .

Shanghai, China, has the world's longest subway system. It stretches for 365 miles (587 km).

BRR! IT'S COLD! TOO BAD I CAN'T TAKE THIS SUBWAY DOWN TO ARGENTINA.

Finland

HOW'S IT GOING ALL THE WAY UP NORTH?

Argentina

The world's most northern subway is in Helsinki, Finland. The most southern subway is in Buenos Aires, Argentina.

# A Huge Improvement

The early subway tunnels in London and New York were made by thousands of workers digging long trenches near street level. This took a lot of time and didn't always go as planned. But the invention of huge tunnel boring machines (TBMs) changed everything! TBMs make it easy to cut through all kinds of ground, from tightly packed sand to extremely hard rock. Today, TBMs are used to dig the world's biggest tunnels. Let's learn more about these incredible tunneling machines!

A TBM has a shield that looks like a large metal **cylinder**. It moves **through the ground to dig the tunnel.**

JAMES WOULDN'T HAVE MADE ANYTHING IF I HADN'T MADE MINE FIRST!

At the front of the TBM's shield, a rotating cutting wheel breaks through rock and soil.

In 1952, James Robbins invented the first modern TBM as an improvement on Marc Brunel's tunneling shield.

One huge TBM spent four years underground digging a four-lane traffic tunnel beneath Seattle, Washington.

NICE WORK, BERTHA!

THANKS, BERTHA!

The TBM that dug the Seattle tunnel was called Bertha. It was named after Seattle's first female mayor, Bertha Knight Landes.

The Tuen Mun-Chek Lap Kok is the world's largest TBM. At 57.7 ft (17.6 m) across, it's wider than the length of a semitruck!

TBMs are also called moles, named after the little animals that dig quickly through soil.

IS THIS GIANT NAMED AFTER THAT LITTLE THING?!

YEP, IT IS!

THAT'S RIGHT! LITTLE OR NOT, I'M THE TRUE TUNNELING CHAMPION!

# I'll Take the Chunnel!

It took 11 TBMs to build the world's longest, most famous underwater tunnel—the **Channel** Tunnel, or Chunnel. The Chunnel was constructed beneath the English Channel, a body of water between southern England and northern France. It takes just 35 minutes for passengers to travel by train through the Chunnel. Along the way, the riders reach a depth of 246 ft (75 m) below the water. Let's hop aboard and find out more!

**Each TBM used to build the Chunnel was as long as two soccer fields.** Two of them were left buried underground!

YOU CAN BUY ANYTHING ONLINE THESE DAYS!

**Construction of the Chunnel began in 1988, but the idea was first suggested 186 years earlier.**

In 2004, TBMs used to build the Chunnel sold on eBay **for £39,999. That's about the same as $73,200.**

The Chunnel is 31 miles (50 km) long. That's about the same as 169 Eiffel Towers stacked on top of one another!

The Chunnel has three separate tunnels. Two were built for trains, and one smaller tunnel was built as an emergency escape route.

Passengers can either ride inside a Chunnel train car or they can sit in their own vehicles, which are driven onto and carried by the train.

# Running the Rails

Want to see more truly terrific train tunnels? The world's longest train tunnel—Switzerland's Gotthard Base Tunnel—runs under the Swiss Alps for 35 miles (57 km). It's also the world's deepest tunnel, reaching 1.4 miles (2.3 km) below **sea level**. In Japan, people can travel by train between the islands of Honshu and Hokkaido at 100 miles per hour (160 kph) through Seikan Tunnel. And there's more!

It took a lot of **concrete** to build Gotthard Base Tunnel—**enough to fill 52 Olympic-sized swimming pools!**

WE'RE GONNA GO REALLY FAST!

WOO-HOO!

**Trains through Gotthard Base Tunnel reach speeds of 155 miles per hour (250 kph).**

THAT'S SO DEEP!

If it's hard to imagine just how deep Gotthard Base Tunnel is, here's some help—**it's 1.5 times as deep as the Grand Canyon!**

Over thousands of years, rain and flowing water naturally carved a passage through Virginia's Appalachian Mountains. **Engineers turned it into a train tunnel named Natural Tunnel!**

NATURALLY!

DO YOU WANT TO COME FOR A TRAIN RIDE?

**Ukraine's Tunnel of Love cuts a path through trees!** The tunnel was shaped by trains clipping off tree branches as they moved along the tracks.

TALK ABOUT A WILD RIDE!

**China's Bund Sightseeing Tunnel uses lights and special effects** to make train passengers feel as if they're traveling to the center of Earth!

YEAH!

# On the Road

Imagine a tunnel so long that it takes 20 minutes to drive through at 50 miles per hour (80 kph). That's the case for the world's longest road tunnel, Norway's Laerdal Tunnel. At 15.2 miles (24.5 km) long, the tunnel passes beneath mountains to connect the cities of Oslo and Bergen. Laerdal Tunnel has made the trip through the mountains much safer, especially during Norway's icy winter! Let's buckle up and check out a few more amazing road tunnels.

The Laerdal Tunnel has lit **caverns** every 3.7 miles (6 km). **Different colored lights are meant to help keep drivers alert.**

I'M AWAKE, HONEST!

**Utah's Zion-Mount Carmel Tunnel has a special system that checks if the tunnel is in danger of caving in. This keeps it safe for drivers!**

Eisenhower Tunnel, which runs through Colorado's Rocky Mountains, is more than 11,000 ft (3,350 m) above sea level.

COOL!

Eisenhower Tunnel was named after President Dwight D. Eisenhower.

THE JOKE'S ON YOU, GUYS!

When Eisenhower Tunnel was built in the 1970s, women were rarely hired as engineers. But Janet Bonnema got the job because her name was misspelled and people thought she was a man!

Bonnema fought for the right to work inside Eisenhower Tunnel. This helped open up more engineering and construction jobs for women.

China's Guoliang Tunnel is another impressive road. Just 13 people dug this mountain tunnel by hand. It took them five years!

WHAT A NICE TUNNEL!

AAAAH! NO, I'M SCARED OF HEIGHTS!

# Mine over Matter

Some of the world's most incredible tunnels aren't used for traveling at all. Mines are holes and tunnels dug into Earth to reach our planet's rich resources of **minerals** and stones. From coal mines to diamond mines, tunnels allow workers to get these important resources. A lot of work goes into planning and building mines that are safe and useful. Let's head down to some magnificent mines!

Chile's El Teniente copper mine has **more than 1,860 miles (3,000 km) of underground tunnels.**

I DON'T SEE ANY TUNNELS.

THAT'S BECAUSE THEY'RE UNDERGROUND!

SO, YOU'RE TELLING ME THIS THING STARTED IN A TUNNEL?!

THAT'S RIGHT!

Electronic devices, including smartphones and computers, are made with many minerals, such as copper and gold. **These minerals come from mines.**

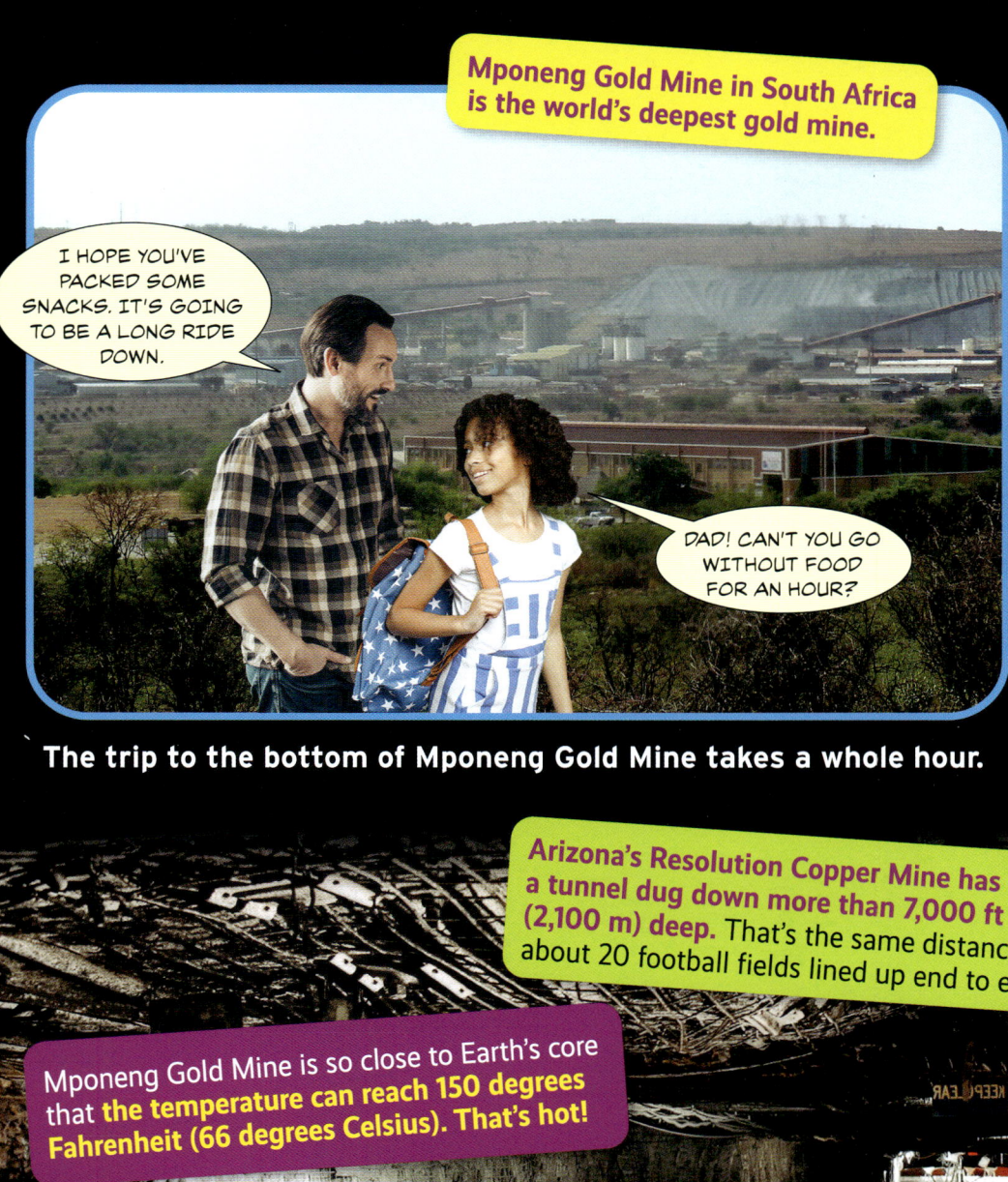

The trip to the bottom of Mponeng Gold Mine takes a whole hour.

# Terrific Tunnels

Where else can tunnels take you? Engineers have used tunnels as parts of all sorts of terrific places. Tunnels make up an underground city called RÉSO, which sits beneath Montreal, Canada. People visit shops, restaurants, movie theaters, museums, and hotels—all without going outside! And in Stockholm, Sweden, subway tunnels form the world's longest art gallery. Some aquariums even have tunnels designed to make visitors feel like they're walking through ocean waters. Tunnels seem to have endless possibilities!

Each day, about half a million people pass through RÉSO's 20.5 miles (33 km) of tunnels.

The name RÉSO comes from the French word *réseau*, which means network.

WHAT ARE YOU DOING DOWN THERE?

I'M NETWORKING!

Tunnels built in Iceland's Langjokull Glacier let people travel through a massive sheet of ice. *Brrrrr!*

THIS IS ONE COOL WAY TO SIGHTSEE!

YES, BUT THESE SOUNDS ARE A BIT SCARY!

**Inside the glacier's tunnels, you can hear the sound of the glacier moving.**

The Atlanta Aquarium in Atlanta, Georgia, has a 100-ft (30.5-m) underwater tunnel where visitors can see sharks and other ocean creatures up close.

HEY! WHAT ARE YOU LOOKING AT?!

Advances in engineering will help us build more awesome tunnels in the future. Someday, tunnels may even be dug and built by underground **drones**.

CALM DOWN, I'M NOT LOOKING AT YOU! I'M ADMIRING THIS TUNNEL!

# Mountain Tunnel

## Craft Project

Engineers have designed incredible tunnels that allow people to travel through many different places, including mountains. Now, it's your turn to design your own mountain tunnel. Use your imagination—and some craft supplies—to travel through a massive mountain. Where will your tunnel take you?

The East River Mountain Tunnel takes travelers between two different states—Virginia and West Virginia.

### What You Will Need

- Cardstock
- A pencil
- Scissors
- Tape
- A piece of cardboard cut to 13 x 8 inches (33 x 20 cm)
- Construction paper
- Glue
- Toy cars

Gotthard Base Tunnel is as long as 21 Golden Gate Bridges!

# Step One

Use scissors to cut a piece of cardstock to 11 x 3 in. (28 x 8 cm). Fold each end in at 1.5 in. (4 cm). Bend the cardstock so the folded ends meet in the center but do not overlap. Tape them together.

# Step Two

Draw a mountain shape on a piece of green construction paper. Cut it out. Use it as a pattern and draw a slightly taller mountain shape on brown construction paper. Repeat with white construction paper. Glue the three shapes together. Place the tunnel shape on the bottom and trace around it. Cut out the tunnel shape.

# Step Three

Cut a piece of gray construction paper the same size as the cardboard and then glue it down. Cut a piece of black construction paper 3 x 13 in. (8 x 33 cm). Tape the cardstock tunnel to the cardboard. Put the black construction paper through the tunnel. Glue it in place.

# Step Four

Place the mountain on top of the tunnel. Push a toy car through the tunnel.

#  Glossary

**archaeologists** scientists who dig up and study old objects to learn about past human life

**catacombs** underground burial tunnels

**caverns** caves

**channel** a pathway through which water flows

**columns** strong poles that support the roof of a building or other structure

**concrete** a hard construction material made from sand, gravel, cement, and water

**cylinder** a shape like a round tube

**diverted** changed the course or pathway

**drones** machines without pilots that are flown using remote controls

**engineering** the practice of using science and math to design and build structures, machines, and other things people use

**explosives** things that blow up

**gravity** the natural force that pulls things toward Earth

**minerals** solid substances found in nature that are not plants or animals

**quarry** a large, open hole or pit used to dig for stone

**sea level** the surface level of the ocean that is used as the starting point for measuring heights and depths

**slope** ground that goes up or down gradually, such as on a hill

**strike** an event during which people refuse to work because of disagreements with their company

**transport** to move from one place to another

**trench** a deep, narrow ditch

# Read More

**Holdren, Annie C.** *Building a Subway (Sequence Amazing Structures).* Mankato, MN: Amicus, 2020.

**Light, Kate.** *20 Fun Facts About Famous Tunnels (Fun Fact File: Engineering Marvels).* New York: Gareth Stevens Publishing, 2020.

**Reilly, Kevin.** *Tunnels (Exploring Infrastructure).* New York: Enslow Publishing, 2019.

# Learn More Online

1. Go to **www.factsurfer.com** or scan the QR code below.

2. Enter "**X-Treme Tunnels**" into the search box.

3. Click on the cover of this book to see a list of websites.

# Index

# About the Author

Catherine C. Finan is a writer living in northeastern Pennsylvania. She has driven through New York City's Holland and Lincoln Tunnels more often than she can count!